Halfway
TO THE EAST

Halfway TO THE EAST

BY MARUSYA BOCIURKIW

VANCOUVER 1999

© 1999 Marusya Bociurkiw

CANADIAN CATALOGUING IN PUBLICATION DATA

Bociurkiw, Marusya
    Halfway to the East
    Poems
    ISBN 0-920999-38-7
    I. Title.
PS8553.O4H34 1999   C811'.54   C99-910076-9
PR9199.3.B558H34 1999

The lines from "Natural Resources," from *The Dream of a Common Language: Poems 1974-1977* by Adrienne Rich. Copyright © 1978 by W. W. Norton & Company, Inc. Reprinted by permission of the author and W. W. Norton & Company, Inc.

PROOF READING
Margarita Miniovich

DESIGN
Zab Design & Typography, Toronto

Printed in Canada

LAZARA PRESS
Box 2269, VMPO
Vancouver, B.C.
V6B 3W2
lazara@web.net
http://www.web.net/lazara

ACKNOWLEDGEMENTS

I am grateful to the many people who read or heard the poems in this collection and gave valuable feedback, in particular Gloria Anzaldúa, Lori Horvitz, leanne johnson, Elaine Littmann, Lori Weidenhammer, and especially, Margarita Miniovich, whose heartfelt editorial comments were greatly appreciated. A wonderful residency at Cottages at Hedgebrook provided some of the writing space and encouragement for this collection, while friends and colleagues across the continent provided shelter, meals and inspiration during gigs and travels. Some of these people are: John Bailey, Chrystia Chomiak and John Paul Himka, Donna Drury, Sheena Gourlay, Jorge Lozano, Lesya Laschuk, Carla Petievich, and Barbara Wisnoski. My grandmother, Jean Wasylyshyn (1906-1998) provided a rich lore of stories and memories—*vichnaya pamyat*. My nieces—Krystyna, Natalya, and Sonya Lloyd—gave me a future generation to write towards. Billie Carroll loved and struggled with me in times of mourning and joy, and gave bountifully of her computer expertise. Zab Hobart of Zab Design was, as usual, a pleasure to work with. Finally, I am indebted to my publisher Penny Goldsmith, who has sustained my work with her vision, her generosity of spirit, and her friendship.

For Billie,
who has travelled with me

Contents

I HEAR THEM SINGING
ALL THE TIME

I HEAR THEM
SINGING ALL THE TIME

hey, hey
> *hey, hey…*

Begin with this

Fields shimmering green with rye
poppies the colour of blood
heat of August heavy as linen on the line
uneasy drone of women's harmonies
moving across the *Pan's** expanse of land
like the coming of a summer storm

keening voice
hungry for freedom voice
wanting an end to misery voice
hardworking voice
mocking voice
laughing voice
longing for sunset voice
wanting
voice

begin with this

hey, hey
> *hey, hey…*

* *"Pan" is Ukrainian for landlord.*

2   (Peace Arch Border Crossing)

> *Skazala shcho vernesh*
> *A schezla na zavzhdy*
> *Oy hirko, hirko mi zhalyu*

> You said you'd return
> But you've left me forever
> How bitter, how bitter is my grief*

My people come from a country
whose name means border
my people have been sneaking border all their lives
smuggling VCRs bibles Marxist tracts dried mushrooms
fake ID vodka software cigarettes and blue jeans
(I was honouring my heritage dabbling in UI fraud
flirting with criminal charges)
the customs officer waved me through with a florid smile
and some comment about our two countries being friendly
not like Those Eye-Ranians who closed the Suez Canal to us
for thirty years   Can you imagine?

Across the room a long line of Asian travellers
waited to have their names tattooed onto a computer screen

What difference then
the length of a room   the span of two centuries
the Caucasus mountains
the pale site of privilege for which my people
were willing to cross so many borders
swallow back so many songs and words

and that other border
the ungraceful power of it
and my great-grandmother's song
like a heartbeat
in my ear.

* *A farewell song sung by my great-grandmother to my*
  grandmother as she immigrated to Canada in 1933.

3 This entire city is for sale:
   city hall entrepreneurs wage war against the poor
   real estate pimps cruise low-rent streets
   TV crews shoot wavering heroin smiles for six o'clock porn
   developers pluck homeless from downtown east side
   like decaying teeth   rain pounds away at cracks
   in rotten condos and bus shelters
   and despite everything you know
   disgrace hits you in the face like a hailstorm
   unemployment insurance border guard taking your name
   landlord taking your money   government
   and poverty
   taking away everything else.

4   (they were slave songs, really)
I hear them singing all the time

hey, hey
                     hey, hey...

landless   rooted
they were singing all the time
in melody and drone
sadness sung with a full voice
like sobbing almost laughter
plangent waves of music
sending messages across the fields

hey, hey,
                hey, hey.

5 Blood on a flag
silence in the archives
history like a headache in your skull.

In 1915 when border crossing was forbidden to Ukrainian immigrants
Petro Marchak, desperate or crazy enough to go across
the Manitoba/us line to look for work
got caught   got arrested   got put in a labour camp

helped build a hotel   a hot springs   and a national park
sang the old songs while shaving in front of a blurred tin mirror
on a 40 below morning in a place where hell had frozen over
tam de didko kazhy dobranich
and even the devil called it a day.

6 Until that moment when harmonies merge in perfect pitch
and hover in the air
polyphonic chords
that travelled the Silk Road to India and back
the air vibrates
poppies leak blood onto the fields
women harvest rye with deadly grace
cornflowers weep
nothing changes
everything changes

and I can tell you:
singing with such sorrow
makes the body glad

longing for freedom voice
keening voice
droning voice
wanting
voice

listen,
the rain goes well with this

> *skazala shcho vernesh*
> you've left me forever
> *oy hirko hirko mi zhalyu.*

HALFWAY TO THE EAST

It had splintered into coloured fragments
when I finally got to see it
east tossed with west   left confused with right

migrant workers from all of Europe's ghettoes
sold trinkets in its absent shadow
a Turkish woman with rows
of Gorbachev / Yeltsin / Brezhnev nesting dolls
tiny Stalins secreted inside
West Germans with faux Soviet military souvenirs
Gypsies with zip-lock baggies of pieces of the Berlin Wall.

I bought a set of smug Matrushka dolls
from a Ukrainian man 3,000 miles from home,
then turned into the whip and spray of rainy late November
like Alice through the looking glass
to stroll into the once-forbidden East:

Blank stone buildings   olive cast of Turkish skin
flash of Cyrillic like gold in a baba's mouth
the phantom cackle of Russian
heard late at night
between the lines of German
on Katharina's radio.

2 In Berlin I was always cold   always shivering
   in dank ashamed museums
   in the stony gaze of Alexanderplatz
   in the sound of German like a gun.

   Accept this cold   said a woman I'd met
   leaning warm towards me in the women's café
   her cheeks the colour of apricots
   then you don't feel it so.

3   Where I live:
edge of British against Asia
temperate rainforest against furious ocean
so different from the east
I thrive like beach grass with succulent roots
so far to the west
east glimmers in a distant mirage.

Where I was born:
frontier town flatlined into wide horizon
an inverted bowl of sky
where the weeping songs of immigrants
in stinking sheepskin coats
stumbling off of cattle trains   escaping slavery
are always in the air.

Where I have not been:
the ancient bedrock of Baba's memory
halfway to the east
impossibly home.

4 In Montreal the streets are where there's heat
   where language weather and colonial ghosts fight dirty
   while cafés breathe with cigarette smoke
   espresso and temporary forgiveness.

   My mouth burned with language
   speaking French was the closest I got
    to fleeing the sound of English like a gun
   but heat consumed my mother tongue
   when I tried to speak Ukrainian
   French words appeared and parched the east away.

5 Like any refugee's child
I dream constantly of being chased   of being captured
of never knowing home
In the middle of the night
that east/west border rises in me
in everyone's nightmare of not knowing where they are
French endearments   Ukrainian curses
English silence
coyote's cry
an old slave song
the rattling hands of a compass gone awry.

ETERNAL MEMORY

ANCIENT CIRCLES IN OUR HANDS

I PALM SUNDAY

We make *pysanky* in vivid early spring
four women around a table
dipping eggs in brilliant primary colour jars of dye
drinking gin   inhaling beeswax
bodies set to the axis of the earth
eggs moving in ancient circles in our hands
I make a yellow/red/green/brown *pysanka* covered in birds
they mean fertility   someone says.

2 Holy Saturday

Branches crack the flat horizon
curved around brown and naked earth
I am in Edmonton embracing familiar and *familia*
the before I was born the after I'm gone
the infinite flow of the Easter egg's line.

I join the straggling niggling family
taking baskets of butter eggs kolbassa horseradish
and Baba's bread to church to be blessed
Baba's too tired today we bring her basket in proxy.
My sister buys candles from the wrinkled man at the door
he's been at that same door since before we were born
candles a dollar each   *you can get them cheaper at Safeway*
I whisper in jest   my sister frowns and suddenly I'm the child
my sister the grownup puts candles in baskets
just like Mama just like Baba used to do
I have no basket   tell myself peevishly you don't bother
if you are lesbian / if you are only visiting /
if you haven't had children.

Priest in nasal voice sings *Khrystos Voskres*
while sprinkling holy water and aiming for the children
they giggle then yawn   candlelight flares
incense swirls around us
song washes over me: water over stone.

3 EASTER SUNDAY

We eat Baba's bread   *it not rise so well dis year*
she jokes: *be careful   you might choke to death.*

Baba tells stories like always
describes Easter *v krayu* / in the Old Country
dere it vas being better system   she says
we brought da baskets Easter morning
then had breakfast all in one day   less trouble dat way.
Baba wants convenience in her tenth decade on this earth
she continues stream-of-consciousness-on
After I be coming here to Canada
I say I always stay in same place and so I have
I never move again.

I who have moved seventeen times in fifteen years say nothing
Baba thinks Vancouver is two hours drive from Edmonton
says it's a good thing her granddaughter always has girlfriends
If you don't marry ees good to have someone   she says
You are smart gerrl.

Baba says next year she might be gone   announces this proudly
like someone saying they're off on a cruise to Barbados
then turns to me and says
You and dat gerrlfriend of yours next year you stay home
get da basket fill it with butter eggs kolbassa horseradish

and da Easter bread   go to da church get it blessed.
Dat way you have Easter yourselves-

less trouble dat way.

FOOD OUT OF ANYTHING

I phone Baba every week now   it's so near the end
time collapses what we have
the weeks have turned to hours.

Baba's bemused by my calls   says there's nothing much to say
the Ukrainian Easter bread she buys at Safeway now
ees so-o-o good with coffee in da morning
the sharp white cold of winter locking her inside
Didn't have no bread no milk for two weeks
What did you eat I ask
When you seen what I seen you make food out of anything
she says   *leettle flour lard potato   dere's a meal.*

It's another Depression now I say to her
those cutbacks that budget
Baba laughs at me with bitter sound   *You don' know
what ees Depression*   she says   *how could you know.*

I tell her about the rain   the mountains
the miracle of daffodils in February
When will you visit   she asks impatient   I don't say
I'm between gigs   can't even afford the no-frills charter
from my city to hers   she makes me promise I'll come soon
she's never made me promise before.

When we're finished talking I go to the cupboard
pull out lentils potatoes garlic onion   *there's a meal.*
Lit candles   cat fed and purring
the walls of the kitchen curving around us
the stars moving with fateful speed
another warm evening against the cold and rain
against the night that may or may not end.

PESACH

The air is full of the tender impossible fragrance of spring
honeysuckle   lilac   jasmine
My lover and I walk through light spring rain to a Seder
room full of difference for me
familiar night different from others for her.

Mother and daughter like scholars debate technique
over roasting chicken   gay men arrive with candies and jokes
I compare Yiddish and Ukrainian
with two older Jewish women
words that swing from the curve of our tongues
round   sensual   impossibly sweet
yes I am Ukrainian I say bracing myself
(the pogroms   the collaborators)
but talk centres on food and language
it's what we have left   it's all we have left
our common heritage
our common loss.

We eat unleavened bread
while a thousand miles away Baba bakes Easter *paska*
we read the Haggadah remembering plagues old and new
boils   locusts   racism   homophobia
we listen to the youngest among us ask ancient questions
while Baba arranges an embroidered *rushnyk*
we use beautiful impossible words like liberation and justice
we taste the salt tears and the bitter herbs.

My father fought fascism and lost
passing on bitterness through blood
this homophobia is my war   a war among my own people
and the words that spill off my tongue in music and in dreams
taste like sweet gone sour   I try not to swallow
don't want bitterness in my body or my life
hide tears that flow at this outpouring of history
this tender new story of acceptance and difference
finding home in this room this Pesach meal.

From bitter herbs we move to sweet
tsimmes kugel and wine
I hold this flavour to my tongue as my lover and I
walk home in a light spring rain
to my brother's sour words on a long-distance line
—*don't come home for Easter.*

We curve into each others' bodies through the night
while Baba dreams of the Old Country
while the earth circles towards light
a night different from all others
a difference from others
a war we share.

GRACE

Sky is a v-shaped wedge of grey
between Douglas fir and arbutus lining the highway
we're seeking grace again
in the last holy week before Easter
bodies set to movement by Baba's sudden silence
and the volubility of the road:
chorus of wind   crescendo of motion
the tumble of place names like candies on our tongues
Gibsons
Roberts Creek
Sechelt
Halfmoon Bay
Madeira Park
Secret Cove.

Grace in the lightness of travelling
the queerness of our passion
the randomness of beauty
the unblinking cool grey eye of a lake
surrounded by burning forsythia
you come around a bend and there it is.

(*Mebbe dis be last time I see you*
Baba always said when we said goodbye)

Grace in knowing that nothing lasts
as though peering through the lake's obsidian eye
you saw the crows' wide-eyed terror
the birch trees' urgent nocturnal fluttering
ecology's web
life's swift current
the ebb and flow of love.

ETERNAL MEMORY / *Vichnaya Pamyat*

a universe of humble things—
and without these, no memory
— ADRIENNE RICH, "Natural Resources"

I   Unbeknownst to you, I had been bringing lovers home to visit you
for many years, you
leading them by hand to the kitchen table:
borscht holubtsi your Easter bread your stories and that last time
when you showed my lover and me
how to make *varenyky*, and the three of us sat round a table
stuffed the dough and talked all afternoon, and I remember
soft gold light suffusing the kitchen like a Vermeer painting
words floating in it like dust motes
(although probably it was just
the flat white light of a prairie summer)
and I remember
that day at least, you were happy.

2   This country stuck in your throat like a fishbone
too new   too wide   you never called it home
the English people you sewed for all your life and you never had
a bad word for them (English words taken on your tongue
like small white pills)
but you always said you wished you'd never come here
that old country tugging on you in your sleep
a spawning ground of dreams.

You've told me about that train ride a hundred times or more,
always that train, from the ship docked in Halifax
to Morinville, Alberta   two young children at your side
this country flashing past in window frames
smokestacks   hayfields   men like scarecrows riding the rails
a dress that stank to high heaven and no money
a Depression no one had warned you about
your hands your stomach empty as dried seed pods
regret filling your mouth like bile
but oh when you got to Morinville didn't your husband look fine
in his Panama hat and double-breasted suit
and didn't you cry when you entered your home
saw pots and pans so new they'd never been used.

Now sleep is the train you take back to the old country
a life flashing past in blurred window frames
sleep your rehearsal for death
your last immigration
and now you say he wasn't such a great husband
and you never knew such loneliness
(French women glimpsed between squares of sheets
hung on clotheslines)
or such cold.

This country
stuck in your throat
crawled under your skin
lodged like dust in your children's mouths
this country broke you.

Only I – hearing your silence –
know how broken.

3   I came to visit you unexpectedly at the slow
    tail-end of an afternoon
    you with a blurry smile that faded when you saw me.
    You'd been watching "Oprah" but ever the perfect hostess
    you turned it off and sat obediently at the kitchen table
    hands folded in your lap
    wistful for television as my words slid past you
    interrupting your schedule: "Dini" at two, "Oprah" at four
"Entertainment Tonight" at seven
    pinning you to earth lightly
    a butterfly still alive.

    I never wanted to live so long
    the only thing you said.

4   Bread is sacred, I remember you kissing
    any piece that fell to the floor.
    I brought you bread at Christmas time
    golden pannetone from Vito's Bakery I thought you'd like.
    Take this and go back to where you came from   you said
    you are not my family.

5   Did you sleep like a cat through the winter?
Did anyone bring you milk eggs and flour?
Every week I tried to phone
but the space between us had gone cold and hard
as the crust of snow outside your window
my voice dancing and quavering upon it like a magpie
scrabbling for food.

(*Why you keep phoning me?*
you said again and again.)

Someone had said it to you: *lesbianka*
a word you'd never heard before not even on TV
you placed it next to the other terrible foreign words you knew
Chinaman Indian Black man
You are not my family you said to me.

6   Last Easter you were still alive
    but instead of going to you we stayed home
    less trouble dat way.

    We made *paska* and *pysanky*
    it took all day
    the sun moved in shadow and light across the kitchen
    the bread rose three times
    my ex-lover came over, said she'd never kneaded bread before
    my lover showed her how: knead till it's smooth as a baby's bum
    it feels alive   she said.

    We decorated the bread with ancient pagan spirals
    the butter with a women's symbol
    filled a basket full of *pysanky* and sacred food
    gunned it to church in the vw van
    the bread still warm   aromatic as incense
    clouds of pink cherry blossoms gusting across blue mountains.

BABA'S STORIES

Yellow summer day
the funeral over
we sit in Baba's dim living room
steeped in amber light the colour of Baba's tea.

All the family outcasts
mismatched aunts and wayward brother
sullen nieces and outlaw granddaughter
flop on overstuffed couches
embroidered pillows in disarray
spilling our ordinary stories.

When Roman used to busk on Jasper Avenue
Baba would ride two buses to put money in his hat
then take him for hamburgers at Eaton's Cafeteria
when Lily slept over Baba would rise in the middle of the night
to check on her grownup daughter
leaning her face close to Lily's to make sure she was OK
when little Krystyna tried to scramble eggs
and burnt them to a crisp
Baba tried some anyways saying *Mmm mmm verry good.*

(*Hmmph* says Lily: *Now we know the cause of death.*)

Liquid with memory we talk
until some of the sad and angry moms
come to pluck the straggling son and drowsy daughters
out of the dying amber light.

The smallest children wheel and deal another night
in sleeping bags
in Baba's yawning house

I see Baba next to the teapot at the formica kitchen table
nodding saying
Nu...chomu ni?
Well...why not?

RIVER

*All water has perfect memory and is forever trying to get
back to where it was. Writers are like that: remembering
where we were, what valley we ran through, what the banks
were like, the light that was there, and the route back to our
original place.*
– TONI MORRISON, "The Site of Memory"

There's a river beneath this street
whispering its watery Babylon
from concrete shores
Pascal's "moving road"
Morrison's "rush of imagination"
a river in a hurry to get to where Leslie Street
meets Lake Ontario   to lose its man-made embankment
to find itself in the long horizon.

There are underground rivers throughout this city
teasing us through sewer grates: their mythic appeal to origin.
There are people working to release these rivers
as though by doing so
they might find the space that history took from them.

I can't stop hearing this river
I know its route
from lines cut into the palms of my grandmother's hands
flowing across St Lawrence and Atlantic

back to Desna and Dnipro
down to Aral Sea
through Caucasus Mountains
Persian Gulf
Caspian Sea
Indian Ocean
curving back for its long journey across three continents
and migrant generations
to Don River's industrial sludge.

Somewhere my father crossed this river
to escape the Nazis
somehow my Baba traversed that ocean
to move into her destiny
alluvial deposits of memory
contain their voices
and traces of gesture
Baba's girlish laugh
her half-English half-Ukrainian prairie speech
the way my father always wore a hat
and kissed the ladies' hands:
the river calls their names

tato
baba
father
grandmother.

Last night it rained
today the river is loud and boisterous.
I dreamt my grandmother welcomed me to her home again.
I know the river cries with me.

STRANGE FRUIT

THE PLACE WE GO TO

The place we go to

is a place without stars
pitch dark

the only sound
the pounding of hearts in our ears

is a place I can't travel to
without you

and yet is neither of our homes
unless home is a place that unsettles
even as it satisfies

is a place that holds
the secret of gravity
the metaphysics of flight

like a rocket's flare
so temporary
so stunning

that in the daytime
my body shimmers
like a field of stars.

STRANGE FRUITS

I   For some reason
I am always bringing you strange fruits
things I've never tried and
don't know how to eat

green figs
yellow papaya
pomegranate
star fruit
prickly pear

as I buy them I imagine
feeding sweet sour morsels to you
one by one
instead it is your mouth that becomes
an entire vineyard
the taste of your flesh more vivid than peaches
I find the fruit
humming with fruit flies
withered and forgotten
the next day.

2   Through a restaurant window
I watch a young woman I know
pick up a peach
smell it
and then exhale slowly blissfully
eyes closed
mouth ripe and smiling.

The next day I run into her downtown
I'm gay she tells me
suddenly triumphantly
like she's won the lottery
her face radiant as summer.

3   It turns out you like ordinary fruit the best
    pears apples oranges
    someone brought us wild strawberries the day
    before you left
    we forgot to eat them
    we had been arguing for days.

    You are gone for the summer
    our relationship a hard pit in my throat
    our love a soft fruit in my belly
    the markets are full of unripened produce
    pale apricots
    rubbery peaches
    green plums

    and mountains of swollen strawberries
    perfuming the air
    I forget you've gone
    I buy too many
    put them in a bowl

    find them the next morning
    weeping red tears.

BREAK & ENTER

I leave the bar early   despite wall-to-wall girls
girls' leather shoulders brushing against me
girls smoky whispering into my ear
girls tangled together
girls wild and alone
rough talking smooth talking not talking girls.

Girls for days: girls
all night long.

But me I was ready to slip away into the mist
where are you *going*
says a girl who's ignored me all evening
and now trails her smart lesbian hand down my back–

–to break into someone's house I say   (she's impressed).

Rain of course and the nocturnal blues of a city
that can't bear to sleep
a bus that slides up like a limo
that glides to her street
I slink along her leafy walk   her privacy
a line I'm about to cross   I'm having misgivings
but I don't turn back

and anyways
I'm full of myself   full of my
femme throat of longing and hungering self
from the black satin bra I wore just in case   right down to the
fishnets and heels I know drive her wild.

Her garden a thicket of weeds she's been meaning to get to for years
and satiny arbutus and tight-fisted rhododendron
soon the poppies will be out
but for now they're fat and fuzzy   obscene wet and green.

I let myself in   don't take off my jacket
or my gloves
walk to the bed
press my body against hers

she's shivering   half-awake
half-dreaming   half-afraid.

I take her right there in my leather hands
and she whispers to me
how before I broke in
she dreamed I was dancing around her bed.

ON READING FREUD'S "FEMININITY"

*If you want to know more about femininity, enquire from
your own experiences of life, or turn to the poets...*
– SIGMUND FREUD, "Femininity"

The cold shoulder of an autumn evening
places our bodies in each other's arms
a book falls to the floor:
Freud mining us for metaphors
our fathers, our fathers
the Other mapped onto our selves
our fathers between us
mine dead yet not
not yet
absent. Leaves illumined by streetlights
fall like yellow snow
if we forgive our fathers for our "inevitable disappointment"
what awaits us then?

My entire body receives your hand
the places that resist
are memory turned inside out
the mine-field of the unconscious
and the electrical storms of memory
like something I hated all my childhood
and now know how it shaped my life

so that I could be here,
at the sharp edge of an autumn night
mouth seeking
poetics of skin
politic of language
even as theory shapes us   even as we resist all theory
to break open the skin of sex
all meaning suspended
as your hand
descends.

RADIO NIGHTS

Once when you were small
you gave away your radio
to a dying kid in a hospital bed
your dad got mad
you didn't get his anger
he didn't dig your generous ways.

Childhood for you
was a covert enterprise
illumined at night
with a flashlight glowing in a bed
the strangers you lived with
raised a tiny adult
how responsible   how polite you must have been;
how secretive and wise.

At night I see you
listening to that radio
sound waves unfurling into the moon shell of your ear
and all the velvety late-night voices
from distant studios and transmitting stations
floating into the safe shoal of your bed
opaque with language
adrift with dark delights of unknown words.

I see you
receiving signals
from the deep blue notes of women's voices

cracking their tragic codes long into a starlit night
beauty and longing and the
complex subterfuge of childhood
a radio that held too much
that solved too little
until finally you passed it
wireless box of illicit treasure
to the kid in the hospital bed.

Your dad got mad
(radios then were precious
not something you'd just give away)
but knowing you now
I think I understand how you –
enamored then as now
with networks hookups
the urgency of unheard women's voices
strategies for sending information on –
would sneak that radio out the house
through swooshing hospital doors
and past the snooping nurses

one kid to another
take this message
and pass it on.

RESTLESS THROUGH
MY DREAMS

Snow, finally, like a slow-moving dream
in this eastern city

eight days before Christmas
the world tilting towards war

cruise missiles streaking light
wreaking their collateral damage:

the unnumbered dead.
I crawl into bed with you after watching the news

craving your heat
our symmetry

the tidal rhythms of breath
too tired

to tell you
that Iraq's been bombed

to ask you
how warheads raining down on minarets

can become as unremarkable
as Christmas lights

to say to you
that I know

how war reverberates across the years
how even unborn generations will hear its tune

to describe for you
how death roars in my ears each night

how my father wanders restless through my dreams
to warn you

to remind you
to mourn with you.

ANYTHING TO DO
WITH ROADS

ROAD TO CHRISTMAS

I Stopping at the Chevron in Langley to get gas
& batteries for flashlights
it's almost Christmas so the guy at the till says
nothin worse eh than gettin' a toy Christmas morning
batteries not included nothin' open 'til Boxing Day.
We play along   *did that happen to you*   I ask
Yup scarred fer life   he grins and then sends us on our way
saying suddenly solemnly   *Good luck on yer quest fer Christmas.*

It's the solstice
we drive the Coquihalla backwards in time
from greenery and sun into brittle wintry night
takeout coffee churns in our stomachs like diesel fuel
a 100-voice Ukrainian choir roars through the van
we're on the road to Christmas
driving into the chill dark heart
of the longest night of the year.

The waitress at Smitty's in Kamloops beams
when we enter hand in hand
voice hardens from treacle into ice as she does a double take
says   *May I take your order* MA'AM
nachos potato skins coffee the bill and it's back on the road
spinning past gabled farmhouses awash with
coloured lights and hope   under wide-hipped starlit skies.

The road to Christmas narrows into vanishing point
VACANCY signs burn holes into the dark
sucking me back into childhood nights
a father driving his family somewhere
on a summer's evening
a mother's frozen silent back
brothers and sisters feverish with children's casual hatred
a daughter's body flushed with all she knows
and does not want to know.

We drive until restaurants flash OPEN signs as red as sunrise
waitresses at Blue River Husky pour coffee like it's mother's milk
we place cold coins into frozen outdoor payphones
say we'll be there soon
road to Christmas sharpens like a knife
mountains resign themselves into foothills
the landscape drags us along
until we get there
the road pulled out from under us
suburban houses and Christmas tree and family
suddenly   so still.

2. *[You measure the crack in their voices*
   the exact pause between your polite comment and theirs
   the razor sharp precision of dishes and forks
   you at the end of the table with your lover next to you
   so tender and concerned   the road pulled out from under you

   the food the bounty and excess of it making you hungry
   instead of full   the smell of fear disgust or whatever it was
   that sat in them humid and fertile for years
   now pungent and glad in the air   and these are your people and

   everything so razor sharp and still]

3 Prairie sunrise flares neon pink in rearview mirror
blue smoke from burning piles of timber
rises from brown and frozen hills
the roads so holy with emptiness
we can't find an open doughnut shop to save our lives
choirs of angels crackle static on the radio
it takes the place of talking
so we leave it on.

All my childhood is on this prairie
signs for ice cream hotdogs beaches campgrounds
ghostlike along the road
this landscape a poem learnt by rote and since forgotten
less familiar yet more mine
than it has ever been.

Clouds stately with indigo lift
like old-fashioned cinema curtains
onto mountains glittering like a Paramount movie
and the road expands with light
the quest continues   we say to each other in sci-fi voices
leaving behind the broken heart of family
moving towards the unsteady promise of community
VACANCY signs flash blearily in broad daylight
ancestral voices moan in a tail wind
urging us home.

ANYTHING
TO DO WITH ROADS

Each year as summer drones toward a close
you and I we get a craving for the road
load the car with tents and maps and Ferron tapes
and leave this town

no real destination
the road's the thing
and anything to do with roads:
truck stops
rest stops
self serves
fruit stands
giant peaches
roadside shrines
pie & coffee
ham 'n eggs
roadmaps
road signs
and any hurtin' song
that sings about the road

days go by
car gets hot
campsites start to look alike
we tell each other stories

from the furthest corners of our lives
(most of which we've heard before)

I phone home
to say
we're somewhere
in Montana
where gin & tonics retail for a dollar
all the bars are called saloons
and vigilantes cruise the back roads
innocent tough and young.

I send postcards
saying nothing much

and when we're back we look at snapshots
that look the same each year
the road's the thing
that and the passion of our writing lives
the restless pull
of maps
and dreams
the healing
narrative line
of roads.

AMERICAN HIGHWAYS

are so privatized
they're almost personal:

Live Work Play in Useless Bay
Please Don't Drink & Drive in Memory of Brian
Ladies of the Beach Adopt-A-Highway Litter Control
Love God Love Neighbour It's That Simple
Thanks Ann We Love You Sunday Church 8 & 10
Apple Maggot Spraying Area
Prejudice Is The Child of Ignorance
We Paint Houses
Jesus Is Our Savior
Mount Baker Highway Future Widening: Call For Info
Whoa There Ya Dang Near Missed Us
No One Is Friendless Who Has A Church
If You Lived Here
You'd Be Home Now.

TO TRAVEL WITH YOU

I dreamed you went back to Africa and I followed you
I had no guidebook   I'd lost my passport
hadn't learnt the language   but didn't want to lose you
so followed you   anyway.

There are things I want to ask but rarely do
in the questions lie continental drifts
of difference and diaspora
where one of us might disappear.
Come with me to India and Africa   you said that spring
it wasn't a dream   you weren't joking
it never really occurred to me to go.

But this is the summer your ma has died
I ask questions doggedly across a long August afternoon
I can't tell where or how your grief has lodged
and I am of the West where talking not silence is a holy cure
I ask questions:
about her about you
about mourning rituals   about family   about feelings.

You tell me everything except your feelings
how you mourned for forty days
how you washed her body and hennaed her hands
how you never cried   how it's her smell you miss most of all.

I bring you fragrant sage from Osoyoos
raspberry jam from Keremeos
salad and blackberry pie
do what my ma would do to make the hurting go away.
My mother will follow yours someday
I am afraid of losing her   I am afraid of losing you

But I wanted to tell you this:
that in my dream I was ready to travel with you
even if I didn't have the words.

HUNDRED YARD
STRETCH OF ROAD

On warm summer nights he plays the banjo
you can hear sweet music all along the old dirt road
that curves between his place and mine
I ask around the neighbourhood   *who's the banjo player*
people smile thinly and look away.

I look out the kitchen window of this house I'm renting all summer
a peaceful hideaway of mountains and mist
for the first time I notice what I didn't want to see
CHILD MOLESTER
spray-painted on the hood of a truck half-hidden by trees.

He did it right here in this house
says the woman living across the road *I've felt the energy*
ever since I moved in   Great: she's a child abuse therapist
he's a pedophile   I'm writing a story about incest
and here we all are on the same hundred yard stretch of road.

Next day in the same kitchen I'm cooking dinner
fiddling dials on the radio   "As It Happens"
a female student in Prince George
protested a criminology assignment : Describe the Perfect Rape
later she was beaten senseless
the cops don't have any suspects
claim the wounds were self-inflicted
concussion   bruises on all parts of her body
she was unconscious for days.

Today the mountains are grey water colour wash
between pure white ribbons of cloud
rain beats a comforting rhythm as I write don't write make tea
I don't hear any banjo music
I've turned the radio off
and think how I'd like to shoot the fucker
or burn the place down
then go out in the rain and photograph the truck
parked by the road   surrounded by cedars
huddled against raging sky.

12TH & CLARK

Luba Sweetheart Call Me Back
posted on a Hydro pole
followed by
Luba I Love You Call Me
and then two steps later by
a rough Ukrainian translation
Luba Kokhany Telefonuvaty Nezabarom
in painstaking Cyrillic text
which actually means
Luba Beloved to Phone Soon.

At 12th & Clark
there's nothing picturesque
Shell and Super Save gas stations
glowing in rainy twilight
the Mini Super corner store
a ragged tree
a major intersection.
I imagine Luba
walking home from the Broadway bus
carrying plastic Safeway bags
full of mayonnaise cat food and cereal
worrying about her phone bill
and the guy who done her wrong
stopping when she sees her name
in Ukrainian

beloved Luba just standing there without an umbrella
squinting at a sign on a Hydro pole
the rain pouring down
her hair matted
her groceries tugging at her hands.

And the guy in his damp basement apartment
leafing through a Ukrainian-English dictionary
he found god knows where
so desperate for another chance
that he'll search for the heart of it
the blood and guts of it
the salty taste
the foreignness
of Luba's mother tongue.

As I walk along the four lane thoroughfare
dirty spray from passing trucks
soaking my back and legs
I think
hell I'd *take him back*
and I hope Luba
reconsiders
or at the very least
laughs.

ROAD TO ANYWHERE BUT HERE

Hottest night of the year so we drag the kitchen table out
onto my sundeck overlooking Knight Street
busiest thoroughfare in Vancouver
diesel   trucks   buses   semi trailers roaring beneath us
while we eat barbecued chicken with our hands
wave wasps away with dishtowels
pass the pickles and potato salad
my best friend me and my childhood pal
who's visiting from out east.

Sweetest night of the year
no car to get out of town or even as far as Jericho Beach
candlelight turns our faces gold as sunset on the ocean
gin & tonics flow like water
we spit lychee pits onto the freeway
and flow easily between three languages:
Ukrainian French and English last of all
I pull out the Scrabble board and the cheating gets more creative
as the gin gets low
as the night cools down
m-o-z-z is short for mozzarella
oj is common usage for a murderer in LA
bi isn't in the dictionary due to homophobia
and therefore it's legit.

The wasps die down and words and all our languages
spark like fireflies in the air
home is where you least expect it
here on this deck with women I love
now in this moment where staying
is a word I long to know and have
there in that place where moving vans bound for
anywhere but here
taunt us all night long.

MARUSYA BOCIURKIW

Marusya Bociurkiw is a Vancouver-based media artist, author, and academic. She is the author of the short story collection, *The Woman Who Loved Airports* . Her writing has been widely anthologized in such collections and journals as *The Journey Prize Anthology*, *Queer Looks*, *Fireweed*, *Border/Lines*, and the recent *Two Lands, New Vision: Stories from Canada and Ukraine*.

Bociurkiw has been producing films and videos in Canada for the past fifteen years, including *Bodies in Trouble*, *Nancy Drew and the Mystery of the Haunted Body*, and most recently, *Unspoken Territory*, a look at lost and 'unspoken' colonial moments in Canadian history. Her works have screened in North America, Europe, Asia and Australia.

Born in Alberta of Ukrainian descent, Bociurkiw has taught at Concordia University, University of British Columbia and Simon Fraser University. She lectures frequently on issues of queer representation and popular culture.